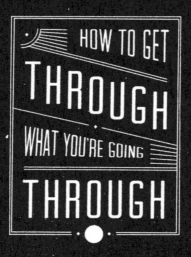

HOW TO GET
THROUGH
WHAT YOU'RE GOING
THROUGH

PASTOR RICK'S
DAILY HOPE

HOW TO GET THROUGH WHAT YOU'RE GOING THROUGH
Small Group Study Guide Version 1.0

Copyright © 2017 Rick Warren

PASTOR RICK'S
DAILY HOPE

30021 Comercio, Rancho Santa Margarita, CA 92688 - PastorRick.com

ISBN: 978-1-4228-03363-3
Printed and bound in the United States of America.

CONTENTS

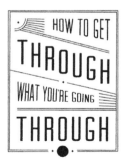

HOW TO USE THIS VIDEO CURRICULUM

Here is a brief explanation of the features of this study guide.

CHECKING IN:

You will open each meeting with an opportunity for everyone to check in with each other about how you are doing with the weekly assignments. Accountability is a key to success in this study!

KEY VERSE:

Each week you will find a key verse or Scripture passage for your group to read together. If someone in the group has a different translation, ask them to read it aloud so the group can get a bigger picture of the meaning of the passage.

VIDEO LESSON:

There is a video lesson for the group to watch together each week. Fill in the blanks in the lesson outlines as you watch the video, and be sure to refer back to these outlines during your discussion time.

DISCOVERY QUESTIONS:

Each video segment is complemented by several questions for group discussion. Please don't feel pressured to discuss every single question. There is no reason to rush through the answers. Give everyone ample opportunity to share their thoughts. If you don't get through all of the discussion questions, that's okay.

PUTTING IT INTO PRACTICE:

This is where the rubber meets the road. We don't want to be just hearers of the Word. We also need to be doers of the Word (James 1:22). These assignments are application exercises that will help you put into practice the truths you have discussed in the lesson.

PRAYER DIRECTION:

At the end of each session you will find suggestions for your group prayer time. Praying together is one of the greatest privileges of small group life. Please don't take it for granted.

A TIP FOR THE HOST

The study guide material is meant to be your servant, not your master. The point is not to race through the sessions; the point is to take time to let God work in your lives. Nor is it necessary to "go around the circle" before you move on to the next question. Give people the freedom to speak, but don't insist on it. Your group will enjoy deeper, more open sharing and discussion if people don't feel pressured to speak up.

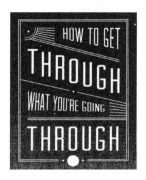

SESSION 1:
SHOCK — When Your World Collapses

CHECKING IN:

If this is your first time meeting as a group, or if you have any new group members, take a few minutes to introduce yourselves.

When did something unexpected happen that literally brought you to your knees? Share how you felt, who showed up, and how you got through the initial stage of shock.

KEY VERSE:

By helping each other with your troubles,
you truly obey the law of Christ.

GALATIANS 6:2 (NCV)

▶ **START VIDEO LESSON**

People can never predict when hard times might come. Like fish in a net or birds in a trap, people are caught by sudden tragedy.

ECCLESIASTES 9:12 (NLT)

"A horrible and shocking thing has happened."

JEREMIAH 5:30A (NLT)

I sat among them for seven days, shocked at what had happened to me.

EZEKIEL 3:15B (CEV)

I'm in terrible pain . . . I'm shocked and hurt so much that I can't hear or see. My head spins . . . Early evening, my favorite time, has become a nightmare.

ISAIAH 21:3-4 (CEV)

I am in total darkness, like someone long dead. I have given up all hope, and I feel numb all over.

PSALM 143:3B-4 (CEV)

By helping each other with your troubles, you truly obey the law of Christ.

GALATIANS 6:2 (NCV)

HOW TO HELP A FRIEND IN SHOCK

1.) _____SHOW UP_____

> When Job's three friends . . . heard about all the
> troubles that had come upon him, they set out from
> their homes and met together by agreement to go
> and sympathize with him and comfort him
>
> **JOB 2:11 (NIV)**

2.) _Share their pain_

> When they saw him from a distance, they could
> hardly recognize him; they began to weep aloud,
> and they tore their robes and sprinkled dust on their
> heads. Then they sat on the ground with him for
> seven days and seven nights. No one said a word to
> him, because they saw how great his suffering was.
>
> **JOB 2:12-13 (NIV)**

3.) _Take the iniative_

> Whenever you possibly can,
> do good to those who need it.
>
> **PROVERBS 3:27 (GNT)**

The greater the grief, the fewer words needed.

2 THINGS YOU NEED TO DO

- ___Cry out to God___

> *"Call upon Me in the day of trouble; I shall rescue*
> *you, and you will honor Me."*
>
> **PSALM 50:15 (NASB)**

> *Get up, cry out in the night . . . Pour out your heart*
> *like water in prayer to the Lord. Lift up your hands in*
> *prayer to him.*
>
> **LAMENTATIONS 2:19A (NCV)**

- ___Let others help you___

> *A friend loves at all times,*
> *and a brother is born for adversity.*
>
> **PROVERBS 17:17 (ESV)**

- <u>Cultivate Stronger relationships</u>

> *Two can accomplish more than twice as much as one . . . If one falls, the other pulls him up; but if a man falls when he is alone, he's in trouble . . . And one standing alone can be attacked and defeated, but two can stand back-to-back and conquer; three is even better, for a triple-braided cord is not easily broken.*
>
> **ECCLESIASTES 4:9-12 (TLB)**

- <u>Grow spiritual Roots</u>

> *"But blessed are those who trust in the LORD and have made the LORD their hope and confidence. They are like trees planted along a riverbank, with roots that reach deep into the water. Such trees are not bothered by the heat or worried by long months of drought. Their leaves stay green, and they never stop producing fruit."*
>
> **JEREMIAH 17:7-8 (NLT)**

> *Just as you trusted Christ to save you, trust him, too, for each day's problems; live in vital union with him. Let your roots grow down into him and draw up nourishment from him. See that you go on growing in the Lord, and become strong and vigorous in the truth.*
>
> **COLOSSIANS 2:6-7A (TLB)**

DISCOVERY QUESTIONS:

1.) Pastor Rick teaches that the most important thing we can do when a friend is in shock is to show up. He calls this the *ministry of presence.* This is a proactive, intentional act of love. You don't wait for an invitation; you act. Share your experience giving or receiving the *ministry of presence* and what you learned from it.

_____

_____

_____

2.) Often sharing in a person's deep pain doesn't require you to speak. In fact, the greater the grief the fewer words needed. Romans 12:15b tells us to *"weep with those who weep"* (ESV). When was the last time you comforted a friend with tears instead of words?

_____

_____

_____

3.) Taking the initiative to help a friend or loved one in shock is the best way to show up and offer support in a critical situation. They simply don't have the capacity to think about and ask for what they need. They are in shock and barely hanging on. Talk about some of the practical ways you can care for them.

_____

_____

_____

4.) When catastrophe comes, Psalm 50:15 teaches us to cry out to God, and in doing so, we honor him. God wants us to lean on him and accept help from others. On a scale of 0-10, how easy is this for you to do?

_____

_____

_____

"Call upon Me in the day of trouble; I shall rescue you, and you will honor Me."

PSALM 50:15 (NASB)

PUTTING IT INTO PRACTICE:

What can you do to start cultivating deeper relationships? You need a safety net of friends who will show up when life delivers the unexpected. This week, think about the people in your small group and how you can start to grow deeper spiritual roots together.

PRAYER DIRECTION:

Discuss how your group wants to approach prayer during this study. Encourage everyone to share ideas. Talk about how this study may make some people feel more vulnerable. Remind each other that your group is a safe and confidential place to share your experiences.

Close in prayer, thanking Jesus for being our wounded healer and asking that the Holy Spirit be ever-present in your hearts and minds as together you learn how to lean on him to get through the tough times.

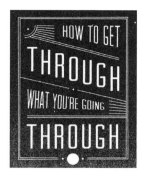

SESSION 2:
SORROW — Getting Through Life's Losses

CHECKING IN:

This past week, what ideas did you think of that will help cultivate deeper relationships? How can you strengthen your safety net of friends who will show up when life delivers the unexpected? Let everyone share and then make a commitment to putting a few of them into practice throughout this series.

KEY VERSE:

The LORD is close to the brokenhearted and saves those who are crushed in spirit.

PSALM 34:18 (NIV)

▶ START VIDEO LESSON

5 THINGS I'VE LEARNED ABOUT GRIEF

1.) **Loss is unavoidable but** grief is a choice

2.) **Grief is** Healthy

• Grief is God's tool for you getting through the
transitions of life.

> *Jesus saw her weeping, and he saw how the people*
> *with her were weeping also; his heart was touched,*
> *and he was deeply moved . . . Jesus wept. "See how*
> *much he loved him!" the people said.*

JOHN 11:33, 35-36 (GNT)

2 UNHEALTHY REACTIONS TO GRIEF

Repression: Unconsciously trying to block out painful thought

Suppression: Consciously trying to block out painful thoughts

If I don't let it out in healthy ways,
I'm going to act it out in unhealthy ways.

3.) **God grieves** with me

> *The LORD is close to the brokenhearted and saves*
> *those who are crushed in spirit.*

PSALM 34:18 (NIV)

4.) Grief is _healed in community_

> *Carry each other's burdens, and in this way*
> *you will fulfill the law of Christ.*

GALATIANS 6:2 (NIV)

> *When others are happy, be happy with them.*
> *If they are sad, share their sorrow.*

ROMANS 12:15 (TLB)

5.) Grief _takes time_

You don't _get over grief_ ;
you get _through_ .

4 THINGS TO HELP YOU GET UNSTUCK

1. _List the losses_ **you've never grieved.**

   Loss of son

   Loss of parents

   Loss of husband

> *"Blessed are those who mourn,*
> *for they will be comforted."*

MATTHEW 5:4 (NIV)

> *Even though I walk through the valley of the shadow*
> *of death, I will fear no evil, for you are with me.*

PSALM 23:4A (ESV)

2. _Identify_ what you've really lost.

a child

Wisdom of parents

husbands companionship

3. Have the _Courage to lament_.

LAMENT: a passionate expression of grief to God; an act of worship that can include arguing or complaining to God.

4. Ask Jesus to _heal my broken heart_.

The LORD is like a father to his children,
tender and compassionate to those who fear him.
For he knows how weak we are.

PSALM 103:13-14A (NLT)

"He has sent me to heal the brokenhearted."

LUKE 4:18B (TLB)

DISCOVERY QUESTIONS:

1.) Processing grief is absolutely essential and is the healthiest choice when you experience a loss. In fact, Pastor Rick taught that grief is God's tool to get you through the transitions of life. Do you have an unresolved loss that is keeping you stuck?

Jims death

2.) Grief is healed in community. People share each other's sorrows through loss. If you have experienced this kind of deep connection with others, please share your reflections with the group.

Shirleys' dad
Kristens best friend

3.) Unmourned losses are like a deep wound that has never been cleaned out, treated, and healed. Left unresolved, this wound can create chronic illness in your body. Does anyone want to share a testimony about this?

4.) Fear is paralyzing, not grief itself. Moving through the grief process will actually help you get on with the rest of your life. Start shrinking your fears by bringing them out into the open in the safety of your group.

5.) You can only get through your pain once you acknowledge it, accept it, and feel it. One of the first steps to help yourself move forward is to list the losses you haven't yet grieved. What emotions bubble up when you think of making that list? Ask your group to support you as you plan to take this first step in uncovering your unmourned losses.

_____

_____

_____

PUTTING IT INTO PRACTICE:

Start reading through the book of Psalms. Get a modern translation, and underline every verse that you identify with and every verse that encourages you. Then you'll have it as a go-to resource for yourself and to share with others when they need it.

PRAYER DIRECTION:

Pastor Rick taught us how to lament. This is simply the act of expressing our grief to God, but it's essential to moving forward through grief. As you close in prayer, thank God for providing this intimate worship experience that allows us to release painful memories and draw strength from our compassionate Creator.

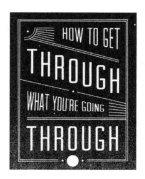

SESSION 3:
STRUGGLE — When Life Makes No Sense

CHECKING IN:

If you started reading through the book of Psalms, were you able to use it as a go-to resource this week? Share some of the verses that you identified with or that encouraged you.

If you haven't started, plan to set aside a few minutes each day to read through the book of Psalms. It could be during your quiet time or before you go to bed each night.

KEY VERSE:

"[Because you sinned] . . .
all your life you will struggle."

GENESIS 3:17B (NLT)

▶ START VIDEO LESSON

3 WAYS WE STRUGGLE

1. We struggle with _other people_.

2. We struggle _with ourselves_

> *I don't really understand myself, for I want to do*
> *what is right, but I don't do it. Instead,*
> *I do what I hate . . . when I want to do what is right,*
> *I inevitably do what is wrong. I love God's law with*
> *all my heart. But there is another power within me*
> *that is at war with my mind.*
>
> **ROMANS 7:15, 21B-23A (NLT)**

3. But our real struggle is _with God_

2 REASONS WE STRUGGLE WITH GOD:

- *We doubt his wisdom*
- *We want to be in control*

LIFE IS A STRUGGLE

JACOB'S EXAMPLE

As a man he [Jacob] struggled with God.

HOSEA 12:3B (NIV)

After he [Jacob] had sent them [his family] across the stream, he sent over all his possessions. So Jacob was left alone, and a man [God] wrestled with him till daybreak.

GENESIS 32:23-24 (NIV)

When the man saw that he could not overpower him, he touched the socket of Jacob's hip so that his hip was wrenched as he wrestled with the man. Then the man said, "Let me go, for it is daybreak." But Jacob replied, "I will not let you go unless you bless me."

GENESIS 32:25-26 (NIV)

"What is your name?" the man asked. "Jacob," he answered. The man said, "Your name will no longer be Jacob. You have struggled with God and with men, and you have won; so your name will be Israel."

GENESIS 32:27-28 (GNT)

God does his deepest work in your life in your identity.

Then he blessed him there. So Jacob called the place Peniel saying, "It is because I saw God face to face, and yet my life was spared."

GENESIS 32:29B-30 (NIV)

Casting all your cares . . . on Him,

for He cares about you.

1 PETER 5:7 (AMP)

THE BIBLICAL PATTERN OF LAMENT

C omplain

A ppeal

R emind

E xpress

WHAT TO DO WHEN I AM IN A STRUGGLE WITH GOD

1. **Tell God what I think is** unfair or painful.

I've lost all hope, so what if God kills me? I am going to state my case to him . . . Listen to my words of explanation. I am ready to state my case, because I know I am in the right. Are you coming to accuse me, God? . . . Speak first, O God, and I will answer. Or let me speak, and you answer me. What are my sins? What wrongs have I done? What crimes am I charged with? Why do you avoid me? Why do you treat me like an enemy? Are you trying to frighten me? I'm nothing but a leaf; you are attacking a piece of dry straw.

JOB 13:15, 17-19A, 22-25 (GNT)

2 KEYS TO LAMENTING

- Complain to God; not about God
- Complain in faith

2. Appeal to Gods nature.

3. Remind God of what he said

> Then Jacob prayed, "O God of my grandfather
> Abraham and my father, Isaac — O LORD, you told
> me to return to my land and to my relatives, and you
> promised to treat me kindly. I am not worthy of all
> the faithfulness and unfailing love . . . O LORD,
> please rescue me from my brother, Esau. I am afraid
> that he is coming to kill me . . . But you promised to
> treat me kindly and to multiply my descendants."

GENESIS 32:9-12A (NLT 1996)

4. Express my total trust in God

> Even though the fig trees have no blossoms, and
> there are no grapes on the vine; and even though
> the olive crop fails, and the fields lie empty and
> barren; and even though the flocks die in the
> fields, and the cattle barns are empty, yet I will still
> rejoice in the LORD! I will be joyful in the God of my
> salvation. The Sovereign LORD is my strength!

HABAKKUK 3:17-19A (NLT)

DISCOVERY QUESTIONS:

1.) Even though we struggle with other people and ourselves, our real struggle is with God. We doubt his wisdom and want to be in control. Why does God love it when we wrestle with him like Jacob did?

_____

_____

_____

2.) God does his deepest work in your life in *your identity*. When he can change the way you see yourself, it changes you. In what way has God helped you see yourself differently? How has that impacted your life?

_____

_____

_____

3.) Is "lamenting" a familiar concept to you? Which step in *The Biblical Pattern of Lament* is the most difficult for you to do? Which one is the easiest? Why?

_____

_____

_____

4.) You can lament out of anger, frustration, fatigue, anger, disappointment, or even fear. What are you tired of tolerating in your life that you need to turn into a lament?

_____

_____

_____

5.) When beginning a lament with something that is painful, it's important to complain *to God, not about God.* You actually leverage your faith and tell God that you know he will listen. Are you ready to take this brave step?

_____

_____

_____

6.) God makes many promises in the Bible. Share some of your favorites with the group. What promises has God made in the Bible that are important to you, and why?

_____

_____

_____

PUTTING IT INTO PRACTICE:

In this coming week, reserve some private time to be with God and lament using the elements of the CARE acrostic. Accept God's blessing as you surrender the things you don't understand or can't control.

PRAYER DIRECTION:

Express thanks for learning the prayer of lament. Thank God that he cares. Tell him you are grateful that you can cast your cares on him, and release the burden of worrying about the things you can't control. Boldly confess that you want him to be the Lord and manager of every area of your life.

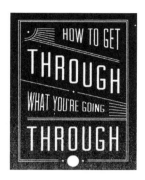

SESSION 4:

SURRENDER — The Path to Peace

CHECKING IN:

Last week we learned that God loves when we lament, when we share our pain with him. Was there a time when you were tired of tolerating something in your life and you chose to turn it into a lament to God? What did you learn in the process?

KEY VERSE:

Everything written in the Scriptures was written to teach us, in order that we might have hope.

ROMANS 15:4A (GNT)

▶ START VIDEO LESSON

DAVID LOSES A CHILD

David begged God to spare the child. He went without food and lay all night on the bare ground. The elders of his household pleaded with him to get up and eat with them, but he refused.

Then on the seventh day the child died. David's advisers were afraid to tell him. "He wouldn't listen to reason while the child was ill," they said. "What drastic thing will he do when we tell him the child is dead?"

When David saw them whispering, he realized what had happened. "Is the child dead?" he asked.

"Yes," they replied, "he is dead."

2 SAMUEL 12:16-19 (NLT)

The Steps of Surrender

1. <u>Accept what can't be changed</u>.

   I can't change it

   • *This is the first step in surrender*
   • *Surrender is accepting the reality*

   David replied, "I fasted and wept while the child was alive, for I said, 'Perhaps the LORD will be gracious to me and let the child live.' But why should I fast when he is dead? Can I bring him back again?"

   New goals, Dreams

   Limbo Land

   2 SAMUEL 12:22-23A (NLT)

   What do I need to accept that's over in my life? *Jims Death*

2. <u>Remember it's not the end of the story</u>.

   "I will go to him one day,
   but he cannot return to me."
   2 SAMUEL 12:23B (NLT)

   Shock, Paralysis

3. <u>Take care of yourself</u>.

   So David got up from the ground, bathed, anointed himself, and changed his clothes.
   2 SAMUEL 12:20A (GW)

   Trust God and do good

4. _Refocus on God thru Worship_.

> *He [David] went to the Tabernacle*
> *and worshiped the LORD.*
> **2 SAMUEL 12:20B (NLT)**

> *I tried to understand all this, but it was too hard for*
> *me to see until I went to the Temple of God.*
> **PSALM 73:16-17A (NCV)**

5. _Do something productive_. *Start moving! one step at a time*

> *Then he went back to his palace where . . . he ate.*
> **2 SAMUEL 12:20B (ISV)**

I don't have to stop mourning to start moving.

6. _Keep on Loving even in your pain_

> *Then David comforted Bathsheba his wife. He slept*
> *with her . . . She became pregnant again and had*
> *another son, whom David named Solomon.*
> **2 SAMUEL 12:24A (NCV)**

> *We know what love is because*
> *Jesus gave his life for us.*
> **1 JOHN 3:16A (CEV)**

DISCOVERY QUESTIONS:

1.) Acceptance is key to surrender. Acceptance doesn't mean you stop caring. Acceptance doesn't mean it doesn't hurt. Acceptance simply means you can't change it. What loss do you need to surrender and accept so you can move on?

_____

_____

_____

2.) Kay shared a simple prayer: *Lord, I believe; help my unbelief.* How does this profound prayer resonate with your faith right now?

___Side by side with God___

___"do things for the Lord"___

_____

3.) The temptation in our grief is to turn away from God. We sometimes blame God because he allowed it to happen. This is a common response. Has something happened in your life that may have caused you to turn away from God? If so, what brought you back into worship with him?

_____

_____

_____

4.) Where is your favorite place to be still with God? Why is this place different from any other?

_____

_____

_____

5.) Grief doesn't paralyze; fear does. What is the one thing that you are so afraid of, it is preventing you from experiencing a path to peace?

_____

_____

_____

PUTTING IT INTO PRACTICE:

Spend time this week reciting the Serenity Prayer:

God, grant me the serenity to accept the things I cannot change; courage to change the things I can; and the wisdom to know the difference. Living one day at a time; enjoying one moment at a time; accepting hardships as the pathway to peace; taking, as Jesus did, this sinful world as it is, not as I would have it; trusting that Jesus will make all things right if I surrender to his will; that I may be reasonably happy in this life and supremely happy with him forever in the next. Amen.

PRAYER DIRECTION:

One person can lead this prayer for your group, or participants can pray this to themselves silently:

God, I am still mourning, but I am going to start moving. I am still grieving, but I want to start growing. I am still hurting, but I welcome healing. Even though I am crushed with this loss, I know I can't change it. I know it's time to surrender and accept. This doesn't mean it's okay; it's just the only way for me to keep moving forward. I trust you to lead me through this. In Jesus' name. Amen.

SESSION 5:

SANCTIFICATION — Transformed by Trouble

Last week Kay reminded us that grief doesn't paralyze; fear does. Was there anything you did differently this past week that released your fear and brought you peace? Share your "peace moment" with the group.

KEY VERSE:

God wants us to grow up . . . like Christ.

EPHESIANS 4:15 (MSG)

▶ START VIDEO LESSON

God's #1 purpose in your life is to make you

_____.

For God knew his people in advance,
and he chose them to become like his Son.

ROMANS 8:29A (NLT)

God wants us to grow up . . . like Christ.

EPHESIANS 4:15 (MSG)

We look at this Son . . .
and see God's original purpose
in everything created.

COLOSSIANS 1:15 (MSG)

1. God uses _____.

2. God uses _____.

"Sanctify them through thy truth: thy word is truth."

JOHN 17:17 (KJV)

3. God uses _____.

4. God uses _____.

We are pressed on every side by troubles, but we are not crushed. We are perplexed, but not driven to despair. We are hunted down, but never abandoned by God. We get knocked down, but we are not destroyed. Through suffering, our bodies continue to share in the death of Jesus so that the life of Jesus may also be seen in our bodies.

2 CORINTHIANS 4:8-10 (NLT)

That is why we never give up. Though our bodies are dying, our spirits are being renewed every day. For our present troubles are small and won't last very long. Yet they produce for us a glory that vastly outweighs them and will last forever! So we don't look at the troubles we can see now; rather, we fix our gaze on things that cannot be seen. For the things we see now will soon be gone, but the things we cannot see will last forever.

2 CORINTHIANS 4:16-18 (NLT)

And we know that in all things God works for the good of those who love him, who have been called according to his purpose.

ROMANS 8:28 (NIV)

3 WAYS TO HANDLE PROBLEMS

1. **Remember that** _____.

- *The secret to handling pain is this: Remember that all pain is temporary but the reward is eternal.*

2. _____ **and** _____.

Give thanks in all circumstances; for this is God's will for you in Christ Jesus.

1 THESSALONIANS 5:18 (NIV)

Rejoice in the Lord always.

PHILIPPIANS 4:4A (NIV)

"Be full of joy at that time, because you have a great reward in heaven."

LUKE 6:23A (NCV)

3. _____.

But let the process go on until that endurance is fully developed, and you will find you have become men of mature character.

JAMES 1:4 (PHILLIPS)

DISCOVERY QUESTIONS:

1.) God's #1 purpose for your life is that you become like Jesus Christ. How is God fulfilling that purpose in your character?

_____

_____

_____

2.) It's easy to love people who love you. But God wants to teach you real love by connecting you with people who are hard to love. How do you see God doing this in your relationships? What have you learned about yourself?

_____

_____

_____

3.) Even though you wouldn't invite trouble into your life, God uses every problem for a purpose. You are transformed by your troubles. What problem are you in the midst of right now? Can you recognize how God is shaping you in this trial?

_____

_____

_____

4.) God specializes in bringing good out of bad. How has he done that in your life? Share how this has changed your perspective of problems.

_____

_____

_____

5.) When you go through a problem, you have a choice. You can pray and ask God to make it easy, or you can ask him to use it for good in your life. Human nature leans us toward "easy," but your faith can anchor you throughout the storm if you trust in God's promises. What promise(s) do you anchor yourself in when trouble comes?

_____

_____

_____

PUTTING IT INTO PRACTICE:

During your daily quiet time this week, read and reflect on the promise within Romans 8:28, which says: *"And we know that in all things God works for the good of those who love him, who have been called according to his purpose"* (NIV).

Practice surrendering whatever problem you are facing as you express your love and thankfulness for everything God is doing to make you more like Christ.

PRAYER DIRECTION:

One person can lead this prayer for your group, or participants can pray this to themselves silently:

God, you bring good out of bad. I trust you and look to you for the strength to keep on going because I know that you have a greater plan. I thank you that you have a purpose for every problem in my life. Help me to understand that purpose. I can't control what happens to me, but I can control how I respond to my problems. Teach me to respond in faith, to be grateful in my circumstances, and to rejoice in you always. Help me to focus on the reward to come and avoid getting caught up in short-term thinking. I know you are building my character to be more like Christ, and for that I am deeply grateful. I pray this in the name of the Father and the Son and the Holy Spirit. Amen.

SESSION 6:

START SEEING — Finding Treasure in Darkness

CHECKING IN:

What did you experience when you surrendered your problems in prayer? Did God reveal something new through his Word as you reviewed Romans 8:28? Did you notice a change in how you responded to life circumstances? Share your thoughts with the group.

▶ START VIDEO LESSON

VERSES ABOUT DARKNESS

*"He wrapped himself in a trenchcoat
of black rain-cloud darkness."*

2 SAMUEL 22:12 (MSG)

*"God has blocked my path and turned
my light to darkness."*

JOB 19:8 (TLB)

*Answer me, O Lord my God;
give me light in my darkness lest I die.*

PSALM 13:3 (TLB)

*"I will give you hidden treasures, riches
stored in secret places, so that you may know
that I am the Lord, the God of Israel,
who summons you by name."*

ISAIAH 45:3 (NIV)

1. God has __Concealed   Riches__ in the darkness of suffering.

> "But he [God] knows the way that I take; when he has tested me, I will come forth as gold."

JOB 23:10 (NIV)

"Community does not simply happen spontaneously except in rare occurrences when conditions are right. Not even the unique circumstances of catastrophic loss are sufficient to create community. When people suffering loss do find community it comes as a result of conscious choices they and other people make. First of all, it requires a choice on the part of those who want to provide community for suffering friends. They must be willing to be changed by someone else's loss though they may not have been directly affected by it. Good comfort requires empathy, forces adjustment and sometimes mandates huge sacrifices. Comforters must be prepared to let the pain of another become their own and so let it transform them. They will never be the same after that decision. Their own world will be permanently altered by the presence of one who suffers. They are changed because they chose to get involved and to allow my suffering to become theirs. They refuse to give me only a month or a year to return to life as it was for me before the loss. Since they knew life would not be the same for me, they decided that it would not be the same for them either."

FROM THE BOOK *A GRACE DISGUISED* BY JERRY SITTSER

2. God has the _power to intervene_ in our darkness.

> The high and lofty one who lives in eternity, the Holy
> One, says this: "I live in the high and holy place with
> those whose spirits are contrite and humble."
>
> **ISAIAH 57:15A (NLT)**

3. God will be _Close to us_ in our darkness.

> . . . So we could seek after God, and not just grope
> around in the dark but actually find him.
> He doesn't play hide-and-seek with us.
> He's not remote; he's near.
>
> **ACTS 17:27 (MSG)**

WHAT WE KNOW LEADS US _Worship_.

> At this, Job got up and tore his robe and shaved his
> head. Then he fell to the ground in worship and said:
> "Naked I came from my mother's womb, and naked
> I will depart. The LORD gave and the LORD has taken
> away; may the name of the LORD be praised."
>
> **JOB 1:20-21 (NIV)**

- *That he is a good and loving God (Job 10:12)*
- *That he is all-powerful (Job 36:22; 37:5, 23)*
- *That he notices every detail of my life (Job 23:10; 31:4)*
- *That he is in control (Job 34:13)*
- *That he has a plan for my life (Job 23:14)*
- *That he will protect me (Job 5:11)*

Though the fig tree does not bud and there are no grapes on the vines, though the olive crop fails and the fields produce no food, though there are no sheep in the pen and no cattle in the stalls, yet I will rejoice in the L ORD, I will be joyful in God my Savior. The Sovereign L ORD is my strength; he makes my feet like the feet of a deer, he enables me to tread on the heights.

HABAKKUK 3:17-19 (NIV)

TREASURES IN THE DARKNESS

Even when walking through the dark valley of death I will not be afraid, for you are close beside me, guarding, guiding all the way.

PSALM 23:4 (TLB)

You light a lamp for me. The L ORD, my God, lights up my darkness.

PSALM 18:28 (NLT)

Let the one who walks in the dark, who has no light, trust in the name of the L ORD and rely on their God.

ISAIAH 50:10B (NIV)

DISCOVERY QUESTIONS:

1.) Physical darkness can distort our vision, and emotional darkness can distort our perspective. If you have experienced depression, anxiety, or any other mental health issue, even if it was for a season, how did God's Word, and the treasures you found there, give you hope?

_____

_____

_____

2.) Often in dark times, we have to dig for the treasures. It takes extra effort, but it also requires support. Who has come alongside you to help and hold you through a difficult season? Why do you think they made that choice?

_____

_____

_____

3.) We like to fix things. We want to get rid of a problem and then move on. Yet to express compassion is a deliberate choice, and we are most like Christ when we choose to offer the gift of our presence and enter into the suffering of others. Share your experiences of "fixing" versus just showing up to comfort someone who is suffering.

_____

_____

_____

4.) The fact that God "summons us by name" reassures us that God will be close to us even in our darkest moments. How does this truth change the way you think about life's most difficult trials?

_____

_____

_____

5.) Look below at Psalm 23:4. This well-known verse teaches us that God is with us even when we're "walking through the dark valley of death." What testimony do you have of God's presence during a dark time?

_____

_____

_____

Even when walking through the dark valley of death

I will not be afraid, for you are close beside me

guiding, guarding all the way.

PSALM 23:4 (TLB)

PUTTING IT INTO PRACTICE:

Take time this week to reflect on all the ways you can praise God, even if you are going through a dark time. Open your Bible and review the Scriptures that support each truth.

- *He is a good and loving God (Job 10:12)*
- *He is all-powerful (Job 36:22; 37:5,23)*
- *He notices every detail of my life (Job 23:10; 31:4)*
- *He is in control (Job 34:13)*
- *He has a plan for my life (Job 23:14)*
- *He will protect me (Job 5:11)*

PRAYER DIRECTION:

Form groups of two or three, and read the excerpt on page 45 from *A Grace Disguised* by Jerry Sittser again. Pray and ask God to create an abundance of compassion and give you the courage to make the choice to enter into each other's suffering. Ask him to equip you to become a comforter and accept the transformation that comes with that choice.

GREENVILLE
COMMUNITY CHURCH

Building Hope. Changing Lives.

dates to
REMEMBER

 **FEBRUARY 9TH**
6:30 - 8:00 PM

FEBRUARY 16TH
6:00 - 9:00 PM

 FEBRUARY 18TH
3:00 - 5:00 PM

FEBRUARY 25TH
3:00 - 5:00 PM

 **MARCH 30TH**
7:00 - 8:00 PM

APRIL 1ST
Join us for our Easter Services
9:30 & 11:00 AM

GREENVILLE
COMMUNITY CHURCH
Building Hope. Changing Lives.

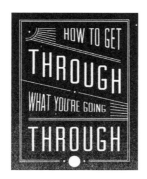

SESSION 7:

SERVICE — Never Waste Your Pain

CHECKING IN:

Last week, Kay taught about finding treasures in the darkness and referenced Isaiah 45:3: *"I will give you hidden treasures, riches stored in secret places, so that you may know that I am the LORD, the God of Israel, who summons you by name"* (NIV). What treasures has God revealed to you during this study? How has this changed your perception of suffering?

KEY VERSE:

Have you gone through all of this for nothing?

Is it all really for nothing?

GALATIANS 3:4 (CEV)

▶ START VIDEO LESSON

5 PURPOSES FOR YOUR LIFE

_____ – Know and Love God

_____ – Learn to Love Others

_____ – Become like Christ

_____ – Serve God by Serving Other People

_____ – Share Your Life Message

Have you gone through all of this for nothing?

Is it all really for nothing?

GALATIANS 3:4 (CEV)

5 WAYS PAIN CAN BE USED FOR GOOD

1. I can use my pain _____.

We were really crushed and overwhelmed . . .
and saw how powerless we were to help ourselves;
but that was good, for then we put everything into
the hands of God, who alone could save us . . .
And he did help us.

2 CORINTHIANS 1:8B-10A (TLB)

I am glad . . . not because it hurt you but because
the pain turned you to God.

2 CORINTHIANS 7:9A (TLB)

2. I can use my pain _____.

By helping each other with your troubles,
you truly obey the law of Christ.

GALATIANS 6:2 (NCV)

3. I can use my pain _____.

Sometimes it takes a painful experience
to make us change our ways.

PROVERBS 20:30 (GNT)

Even though Jesus was God's Son, he learned
obedience from the things he suffered.

HEBREWS 5:8 (NLT)

Suffering made Jesus perfect, and now he can save forever all who obey him.

HEBREWS 5:9 (CEV)

Isn't it wonderful all the ways in which this distress has goaded you closer to God? You're more alive, more concerned, more sensitive, more reverent, more human, more passionate, more responsible. Looked at from any angle, you've come out of this with purity of heart.

2 CORINTHIANS 7:11 (MSG)

We are pressed on every side by troubles, but we are not crushed. We are perplexed, but not driven to despair. We are hunted down, but never abandoned by God. We get knocked down, but we are not destroyed. Through suffering, our bodies continue to share in the death of Jesus so that the life of Jesus may also be seen in our bodies.

2 CORINTHIANS 4:8-10 (NLT)

4. I can use my pain _____.

> *He comforts us in all our troubles so that we can comfort others. When they are troubled, we will be able to give them the same comfort God has given us. For the more we suffer for Christ, the more God will shower us with his comfort through Christ. Even when we are weighed down with troubles, it is for your comfort and salvation! For when we ourselves are comforted, we will certainly comfort you. Then you can patiently endure the same things we suffer.*
> **2 CORINTHIANS 1:4-6 (NLT)**

5. I can use my pain _____.

Your deepest life message will come out of your deepest pain.

DISCOVERY QUESTIONS:

1.) How can people intentionally cultivate deeper relationships — whether in a marriage, friendship, or fellowship group — that will allow them to become vulnerable by openly sharing their feelings and experiences? Share your ideas or real-life experiences with the group.

_____

_____

_____

2.) Our pain can be used to reach out and comfort others. Why would sharing our weaknesses be more effective in connecting with others than sharing our accomplishments?

_____

_____

_____

3.) Winning in life requires resilience: the ability to bounce back from our problems and pains by seeing God's purpose in them. Describe an example from your life that God has used to cultivate your purpose.

_____

_____

_____

4.) Pastor Rick talked about four levels of fellowship: sharing, studying, serving, and suffering. Openly talk about what level your group is in now and how you could make progress toward the next level of fellowship. Share ideas and encourage everyone to contribute to the conversation.

_____

_____

_____

5.) God's #1 purpose in your life is to make you like Jesus. In what ways have you become more like Jesus during this study? In your thought life? Your prayer life? How you relate to others? Share your discoveries with the group.

_____

_____

_____

PUTTING IT INTO PRACTICE:

Think of one of the most painful experiences in your life. Then go back over this lesson and look at how God could use that situation in each of the five ways Pastor Rick shared. Is one or more of these difficult for you to explore? Do you know why?

PRAYER DIRECTION:

One person can lead this prayer for your group, or participants can pray this to themselves silently:

Jesus Christ, use the pain in my life to draw me closer to you, so I can learn how to really love and draw closer to others. Please use the pain in my life to make me more like you. I don't want to waste my pain. I want to use it to serve others, and glorify you. My greatest desire is that you would use the pain in my life as a witness to the world that you can be counted on, that you are a good God, and that you provide strength in every situation — even in the most difficult of times. In Jesus' name I pray. Amen.

HELP FOR HOSTS

TOP 10 IDEAS FOR NEW HOSTS

CONGRATULATIONS! As the host of your small group, you have responded to the call to help shepherd Jesus' flock. Few other tasks in the family of God surpass the contribution you will be making. As you prepare to facilitate your group, whether it is one session or the entire series, here are a few thoughts to keep in mind.

Remember you are not alone. God knows everything about you, and he knew you would be asked to facilitate your group. Even though you may not feel ready, this is common for all good hosts. God promises, *"I will never leave you; I will never abandon you"* (Hebrews 13:5 GNT). Whether you are facilitating for one evening, several weeks, or a lifetime, you will be blessed as you serve.

1. **DON'T TRY TO DO IT ALONE.** Pray right now for God to help you build a healthy team. If you can enlist a co-host to help you shepherd the group, you will find your experience much richer. This is your chance to involve as many people as you can in building a healthy group. All you have to do is ask people to help. You'll be surprised at the response.

2. **BE FRIENDLY AND BE YOURSELF.** God wants to use your unique gifts and temperament. Be sure to greet people at the door with a big smile . . . this can set the mood for the whole gathering. Remember, they are taking as big a step to show up at your house as you are to host a small group! Don't try to do things exactly like another host; do them in a way that fits you. Admit when you don't have an answer and apologize when you make a mistake. Your group will love you for it and you'll sleep better at night.

3. **PREPARE FOR YOUR MEETING AHEAD OF TIME.** Review the session and write down your responses to each question. Pay special attention to the Putting It Into Practice exercises that ask group members to do something other than engage in discussion. These exercises will help your group live what the Bible teaches, not just talk about it.

4. **PRAY FOR YOUR GROUP MEMBERS BY NAME.** Before you begin your session, take a few moments and pray for each member by name. You may want to review the Small Group Prayer and Praise Report at least once a week. Ask God to use your time together to touch the heart of each person in your group. Expect God to lead you to whomever he wants you to encourage or challenge in a special way. If you listen, God will

FREQUENTLY ASKED QUESTIONS

HOW LONG WILL THIS GROUP MEET?

This study is seven sessions. We encourage your group to add a session for a celebration. In your final session, each group member may decide if he or she desires to continue on for another study. At that time you may also want to do some informal evaluation, discuss your group guidelines, and decide which study you want to do next. We recommend you visit our website at **PastorRick.com** for more video-based small group studies.

WHO IS THE HOST?

The host is the person who coordinates and facilitates your group meetings. In addition to a host, we encourage you to select one or more group members to lead your group discussions. Several other responsibilities can be rotated, including refreshments, prayer requests, worship, or keeping up with those who miss a meeting. Shared ownership in the group helps everybody grow.

WHERE DO WE FIND NEW GROUP MEMBERS?

Recruiting new members can be a challenge for groups, especially new groups with just a few people, or existing groups that lose a few people along the way. We encourage you to use the Circles of Life diagram on page 63 of this study guide to brainstorm a list of people from your workplace, church, school, neighborhood, family, and so on. Then pray for the people on each member's list. Allow each member to invite several people from their list. Some groups fear that newcomers will interrupt the intimacy that members have built over time. However, groups that welcome newcomers generally gain strength with the infusion of new blood. Remember, the next person you add just might become a friend for eternity. Logistically, groups find different ways to add members. Some groups remain permanently open, while others choose to open periodically, such as at the beginning or end of a study. If your group becomes too large for easy, face-to-face conversations, you can subgroup, forming a second discussion group in another room.

HOW DO WE HANDLE CHILDCARE NEEDS?

Childcare needs must be handled very carefully. This is a sensitive issue. We suggest you seek creative solutions as a group. One common solution is to have the adults meet in the living room and share the cost of a babysitter (or two) who can be with the kids in another part of the house.

Another popular option is to have one home for the kids and a second home (close by) for the adults. If desired, the adults could rotate the responsibility of providing a lesson for the kids. This last option is great with school-age kids and can be a huge blessing to families.

CIRCLES OF LIFE

SMALL GROUP CONNECTIONS

Discover Who You Can Connect in Community. Use the chart on the following page to help carry out one of the values in the Group Guidelines, to "Welcome Newcomers."

FOLLOW THIS SIMPLE THREE-STEP PROCESS:

1. List one or two people in each circle.
2. Prayerfully select a person or couple from your list and tell your group about them.
3. Give them a call and invite them to your next meeting. Over 50 percent of those invited to a small group say, "Yes!"

FAMILY
(immediate or extended)

_____

_____

FELLOWSHIP
(church relationships)

_____

_____

FRIENDS
(neighbors, kids, sports, school, etc.)

_____

_____

FUN
(gym, hobbies, hangouts)

_____

_____

FACTORY/ FIRM
(work, professional arena)

_____

_____

GROUP GUIDELINES

It's a good idea for every group to put words to their shared values, expectations, and commitments. Such guidelines will help you avoid unspoken agendas and unmet expectations. We recommend you discuss your guidelines during Session 1 in order to lay the foundation for a healthy group experience. Feel free to modify anything that does not work for your group.

WE AGREE TO THE FOLLOWING VALUES:

CLEAR PURPOSE	To grow healthy spiritual lives by building a healthy small group community.
GROUP ATTENDANCE	To give priority to the group meeting (call if I am absent or late).
SAFE ENVIRONMENT	To create a safe place where people can be heard and feel loved (no quick answers, snap judgments, or simple fixes).
BE CONFIDENTIAL	To keep anything that is shared strictly confidential and within the group.
CONFLICT RESOLUTION	To avoid gossip and to immediately resolve any concerns by following the principles of Matthew 18:15-17.
SPIRITUAL HEALTH	To give group members permission to speak into my life and help me live a healthy, balanced spiritual life that is pleasing to God.
LIMIT OUR FREEDOM	To limit our freedom by not serving or consuming alcohol during small group meetings or events so as to avoid causing a weaker brother or sister to stumble (1 Corinthians 8:1-13; Romans 14:19-21).

WELCOME NEWCOMERS   To invite friends who might benefit from this study and warmly welcome newcomers.

BUILDING RELATIONSHIPS   To get to know the other members of the group and pray for them regularly.

OTHER   _____

_____

_____

_____

_____

WE HAVE ALSO DISCUSSED AND AGREE ON THE FOLLOWING ITEMS:

CHILDCARE   _____

STARTING TIME   _____

ENDING TIME   _____

SMALL GROUP
TIMES AND CALENDAR

Healthy groups share responsibilities and group ownership. It might take some time for this to develop. Shared ownership ensures that responsibility for the group doesn't fall to one person. Use the calendar to keep track of social events, mission projects, birthdays, or days off. Complete this calendar at your first or second meeting. Planning ahead will increase attendance and shared ownership.

DATE	LESSON	LOCATION	FACILITATOR	SNACK OR MEAL
	Session 1			
	Session 2			
	Session 3			
	Session 4			
	Session 5			
	Session 6			
	Session 7			
	Celebration			

ANSWER KEY

SESSION 1: SHOCK — WHEN YOUR WORLD COLLAPSES

1. <u>Show up</u>

2. <u>Share their pain</u>

3. <u>Take the initiative</u>

- <u>Cry out to God</u>

- <u>Let others help</u>

- <u>Cultivate stronger relationships</u>

- <u>Grow spiritual roots</u>

SESSION 2: SORROW — GETTING THROUGH LIFE'S LOSSES

1. Loss is unavoidable but <u>grief is a choice.</u>

2. Grief is <u>healthy</u>.

• Grief is <u>God's tool</u> for you getting through the <u>transitions of life</u>.

Repression: <u>Unconsciously trying to block out painful thoughts</u>

Suppression: <u>Consciously trying to block out painful thoughts</u>

If I don't <u>let it out in healthy ways,</u>
I'm going to <u>act it out in unhealthy ways</u>.

3. God grieves <u>with me</u>.

4. Grief is <u>healed in community</u>.

5. Grief <u>takes time</u>.

You don't <u>get over grief</u>; you <u>get through it</u>.

1. <u>List the losses</u> you've never grieved.

2. <u>Identify</u> what you've really lost.

3. Have the <u>courage to lament</u>.

4. Ask Jesus to <u>heal your broken heart</u>.

1. We struggle with <u>other people</u>.

2. We struggle <u>with ourselves</u>.

3. But our real struggle is <u>with God</u>.

God does his deepest work in your life in <u>your identity</u>.

The Biblical Pattern of Lament:

C: <u>Complain</u>

A: <u>Appeal</u>

R: <u>Remind</u>

E: <u>Express</u>

1. Tell God what I think is <u>unfair or painful</u>.

2 Keys to Lamenting:

• <u>Complain to God, not about God</u>

• <u>Complain in faith</u>

2. <u>Appeal to God's nature.</u>

3. <u>Remind God of what he said.</u>

4. <u>Express my total trust in God.</u>

SESSION 4: SURRENDER — THE PATH TO PEACE

1. <u>Accept what cannot be changed.</u>

2. <u>Remember it's not the end of the story.</u>

3. <u>Take care of yourself.</u>

4. <u>Refocus on God through worship.</u>

5. <u>Do something productive.</u>

6. <u>Keep on loving even in your pain.</u>

SESSION 5: SANCTIFICATION — TRANSFORMED BY TROUBLE

God's #1 purpose in your life is to make you **more like Jesus Christ.**

4 Things God Uses to Make You Like Jesus

1. God uses his Spirit.

2. God uses his Word.

3. God uses other people.

4. God uses problems.

3 Ways to Handle Problems

1. Remember that God's plan is good.

2. Rejoice and give thanks.

3. Refuse to give up.

SESSION 6: START SEEING — FINDING TREASURE IN DARKNESS

1. God has concealed riches in the darkness of suffering.

2. God has the power to intervene in our darkness.

3. God will be close to us in our darkness.

What we know leads us to worship.

SESSION 7: SERVICE — NEVER WASTE YOUR PAIN

5 Purposes for Your Life

1. Worship – Know and Love God

2. Fellowship – Learn to Love Others

3. Discipleship – Become Like Christ

4. Ministry – Serve God by Serving Other People

5. Mission – Share Your Life Message

5 Ways Pain Can Be Used for Good

1. I can use my pain to draw closer to God.

2. I can use my pain to draw closer to others.

3. I can use my pain to become more like Jesus.

4. I can use my pain to help others.

5. I can use my pain to witness to the world.

SMALL GROUP PRAYER AND PRAISE REPORT

This is a place where you can write each other's requests for prayer. You can also make a note when God answers a prayer. Pray for each other's requests. If you're new to group prayer, it's okay to pray silently or to pray by using just one sentence:

"God, please help _____ to _____ ."

DATE/PERSON	PRAYER REQUEST	PRAISE REPORT

DATE/PERSON	PRAYER REQUEST	PRAISE REPORT

DATE/PERSON	PRAYER REQUEST	PRAISE REPORT

DATE/PERSON	PRAYER REQUEST	PRAISE REPORT

DATE/PERSON	PRAYER REQUEST	PRAISE REPORT

DATE/PERSON	PRAYER REQUEST	PRAISE REPORT

DATE/PERSON	PRAYER REQUEST	PRAISE REPORT

DATE/PERSON	PRAYER REQUEST	PRAISE REPORT

DATE/PERSON	PRAYER REQUEST	PRAISE REPORT

KEY VERSES

By helping each other with your troubles,
you truly obey the law of Christ.

GALATIANS 6:2 (NCV)

The LORD is close to the brokenhearted and saves
those who are crushed in spirit.

PSALM 34:18 (NIV)

"[Because you sinned] . . .
all your life you will struggle."

GENESIS 3:17B (NLT)

Everything written in the Scriptures was written to
teach us, in order that we might have hope.

ROMANS 15:4A (GNT)

God wants us to grow up . . . like Christ.

EPHESIANS 4:15 (MSG)

"I will give you hidden treasures, riches stored in
secret places, so that you may know that I am the
LORD, the God of Israel, who summons you by name."

ISAIAH 45:3 (NIV)

Have you gone through all of this for nothing?
Is it all really for nothing?

GALATIANS 3:4 (CEV)